This library edition published in 2011 by Walter Foster Publishing, Inc.
Walter Foster Library
Distributed by Black Rabbit Books.
P.O. Box 3263 Mankato, Minnesota 56002

Printed in China by PRINTPLUS Limited, Shenzhen.

First Library Edition

Library of Congress Cataloging-in-Publication Data

Farrell, Russell.
    Learn to draw horses & ponies : learn to draw and color 25 favorite horse and pony breeds, step by easy step, shape by simple shape! / illustrated by Russell Farrell. – 1st library ed.
        p. cm.
    ISBN 978-1-936309-16-0 (hardcover)
    1. Horses in art–Juvenile literature. 2. Drawing–Technique–Juvenile literature. I. Title. II. Title: Learn to draw horses and ponies. III. Title: Learn to draw and color 25 favorite horse and pony breeds, step by easy step, shape by simple shape!
    NC783.8.H65F37 2011
    743.6'96655–dc22

                                                        2010004205

022010
OP1825

9 8 7 6 5 4 3 2 1

Learn to Draw
Horses & Ponies

Learn to draw and color 25 favorite
horse and pony breeds, step by easy step,
shape by simple shape!

Illustrated by Russell Farrell

Getting Started

When you **look** closely at the **drawings** in this book, you'll notice that they're made up of basic shapes, such as circles, ovals and triangles. To draw all your favorite horses and ponies, just start with simple shapes as you see here. It's easy and fun!

Circles are one way to start a horse's head, chest, and hips.

Ovals make good profile heads and muzzles.

Triangles are perfect for upright ears!

Coloring Tips

There's more than one way to bring your **four-legged** friends to life on paper—you can use crayons, markers, or colored pencils. Just be sure you have plenty of good "horse colors"— black, brown, and white, plus yellow, orange, red, and blue.

Pencil

Crayon

Watercolor

Colored pencil

Australian Pony

This **sweet** little pony from "down under" has a **fine**, delicate face and large, dark eyes. Say, "G'day, mate!"

1

2

3

4

fun fact

Because it has a calm personality, responds well under harness, and offers a smooth ride with flowing movement, this Aussie native is a popular child's riding pony.

5

Hackney Horse

This handsome **show horse** is strutting its stuff—
stretch out those legs and arch that tail high!

Hanoverian Foal

Start this **long-legged** baby with two circles for the body. Then finish with a short, brushlike tail and a stiff, upright mane.

5

6

7

fun fact

The first Hanoverians worked as carriage and military horses. But the Hanoverian is now one of the most important sport horse breeds. With their long stride, powerful action, and excellent jumping skills, they have won many world championships, including a number of Olympic medals and more World Cups than any other breed!

Pinto

This **color** breed has a **cool** patterned coat that sets it apart!
A Quarter Horse or Thoroughbred Pinto can also be called a "Paint."

fun fact

Both Pintos and Paints have the same patterns of coloring, so how can you tell the difference between these breeds? Every Paint is a Pinto, but not every Pinto is a Paint. The Pinto registry is less exclusive than the Paint registry.

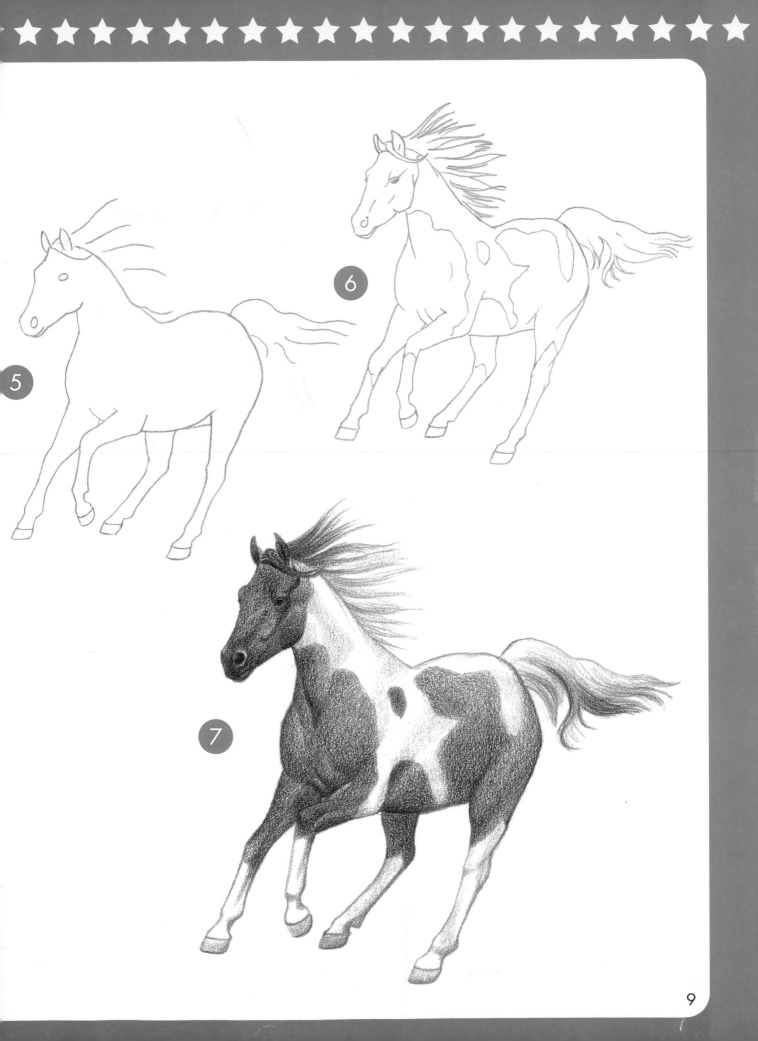

Welsh Mountain Pony

This little **foal** is as cute as can be! First draw its **sturdy,** round body. Then add super long legs!

1

2

3

4

5

6

Norwegian Fjord Pony

This **primitive-looking** pony has **zebra** stripes on its legs and a dark stripe on its back that goes right through its mane!

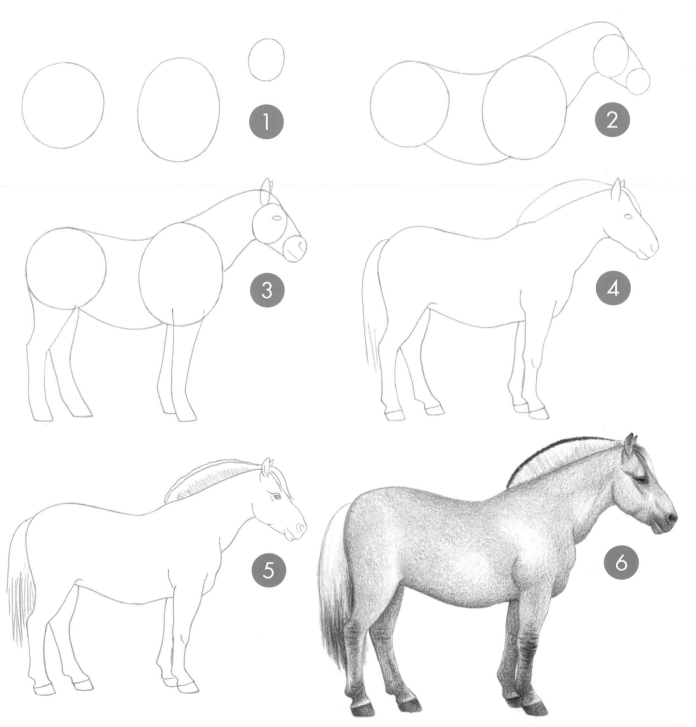

11

Clydesdale

The Clydesdale is a big and powerful draft horse, with long leg hairs—called "feathers"—that almost cover its hooves!

Arabian

Its delicate, **dished** profile, large **eyes** and nostrils, and small, pointed ears give the Arabian a noble and gentle appearance.

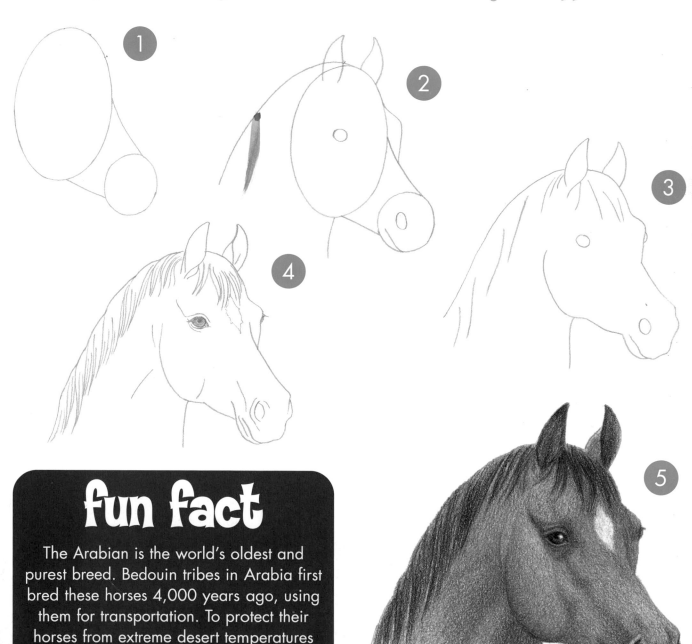

fun fact

The Arabian is the world's oldest and purest breed. Bedouin tribes in Arabia first bred these horses 4,000 years ago, using them for transportation. To protect their horses from extreme desert temperatures (and thieves), the Bedouins kept the Arabians in their tents, sleeping, resting, and eating with their steeds by their side.

Noriker

An **ancient** Austrian **draft** breed (heavy workhorse), the Noriker is strong and stocky, with a long silky mane, tail, and forelock.

American Saddlebred

This **high-spirited** horse shows off its **proud** style with a high-flying tail and a prancing step!

fun fact

The Saddlebred not only walks, trots, and canters—it can also perform two additional smooth, easy-riding gaits: *slow gait* and *rack*. Some horses can carry out the five gaits naturally at birth, but others must be trained to perform the two special gaits.

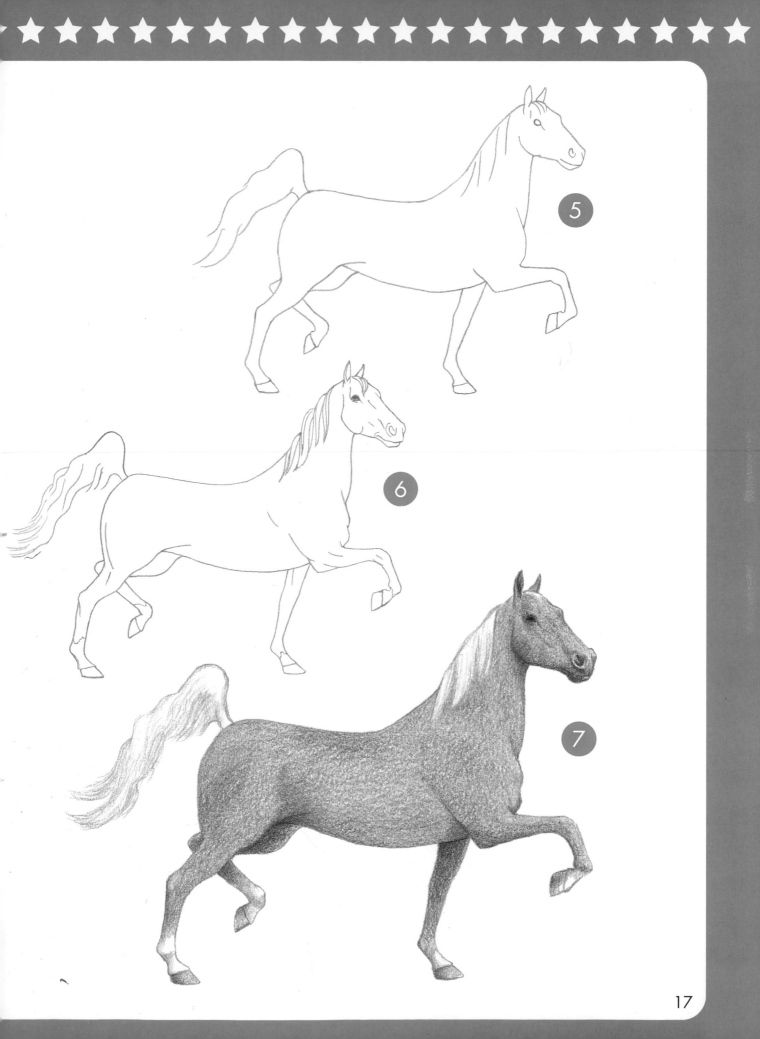

Morgan

Small but super **strong** and hardy, the Morgan has a draft horse's muscular hindquarters but thinner legs and an elegant face.

Thoroughbred

The **fastest** breed in the world, the **athletic** and courageous Thoroughbred can run and jump for miles and miles!

fun fact

Every Thoroughbred racehorse celebrates its birthday on New Year's day. A newborn is considered a foal until January 1st of the year after it is born; then it's called a "yearling."

Horses in Action

Whether **working** or **playing,** horses and people have been partners for thousands of years! Try your hand at drawing these active horses as they run, jump, and show off their skills!

Sliding stop

Racing

Playing polo

Jumping

Dressage

Harness racing

Friesian

Rapunzel would **envy** the long, flowing **locks** of this solid black Friesian—a heavy draft horse from the Netherlands.

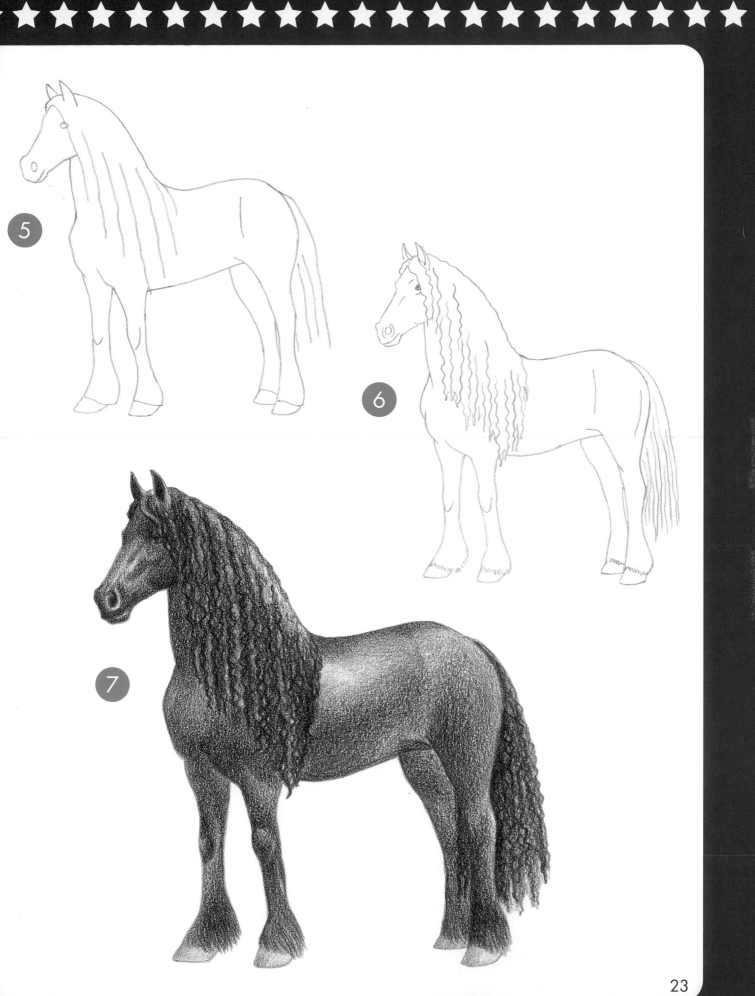

Shetland Pony

A **favorite** breed of pony-loving kids, the **adorable** Shetland is tiny but tough, with a round belly and short, stocky legs.

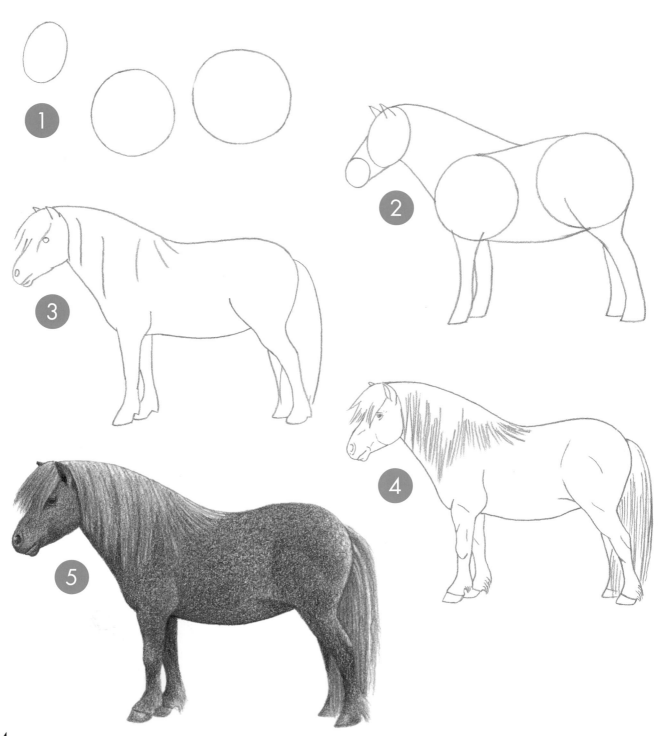

Kathiawari

This narrowly built horse from **India** has distinctive **ears** that curve inward until their tips actually touch!

fun fact

This horse is small, but it's also tough, which is why the Kathiawari is a favorite of tent-pegging athletes. Originally a way to practice wild boar hunting, *tent pegging* is now a popular sport in India. To play the game, an athlete rides to the center of an arena and, while on horse-back, uses the tip of a lance to pick up a small wooden block—or peg. Picking up the peg earns the rider half a point; picking up the peg and carrying it to the opposite corner of the arena earns a full point.

American Quarter Horse

With its **muscular** hindquarters and **powerful** shoulders, this Western horse can sprint like an Olympian and stop on a dime!

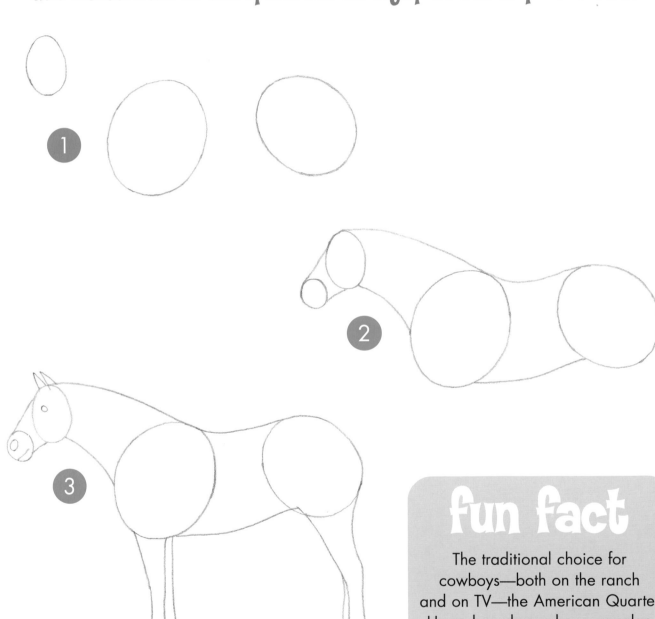

fun fact

The traditional choice for cowboys—both on the ranch and on TV—the American Quarter Horse has always been popular. Now it's the #1 breed worldwide, with more than 3 million entries in the American Quarter Horse Association registry!

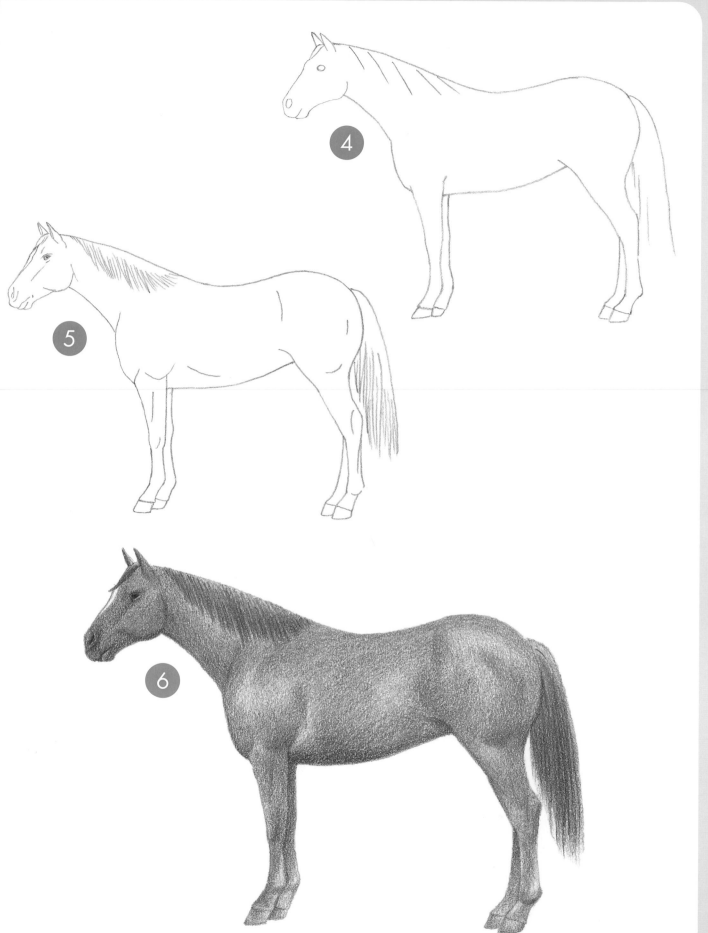

Appaloosa

The **easy-going** Appaloosa is awash in **spots!** Along with its frosted coat pattern, it has a multi-colored tail.

fun fact

The first horses in the United States arrived in 1493. By 1780, most Native American tribes had horses, including the Nez Percé of the West. Expert horsemen, the Nez Percé selectively bred spotted horses, which later became the Appaloosa breed.

Highland Pony

This **sure-footed** Scottish pony has the **build** of a draft horse, with soft, silky feathers on its lower legs.

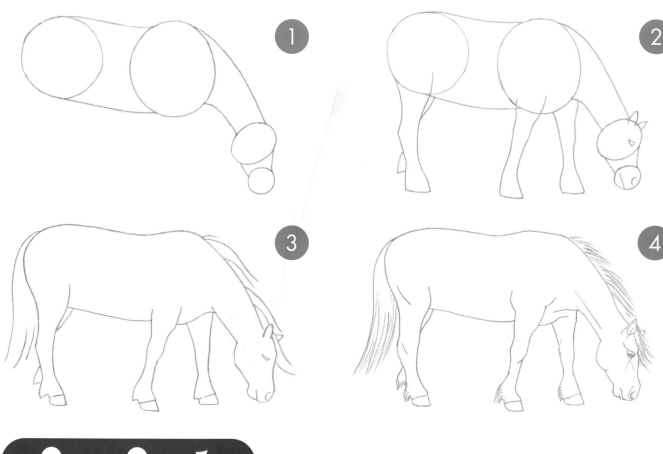

1

2

3

4

fun fact

Highland foals often have "primitive" markings on their coats, including stripes on the back, shoulders, and legs; or dark spots on the mane, tail, and legs. Some of the markings fade over time, but others continue to show throughout the ponies' entire lives.

5

Paso Fino

Also called a "**stepping**" horse for its natural, **lively** gait, the Paso has long hind legs and pasterns and very flexible joints.

Percheron

The **unfeathered** Percheron is a popular **heavy** breed. Despite its size, it has the elegance of its Arabian ancestors.

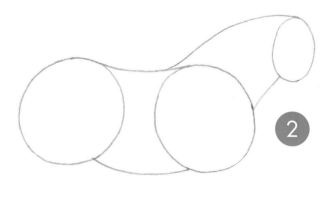

fun fact

Three of the foals recorded in the first American Percheron stud book in 1876 were fathered by a horse named Diligence. Diligence, a native of La Perche, France, arrived in the United States in 1839; once in the states, he reportedly sired more than 400 foals!

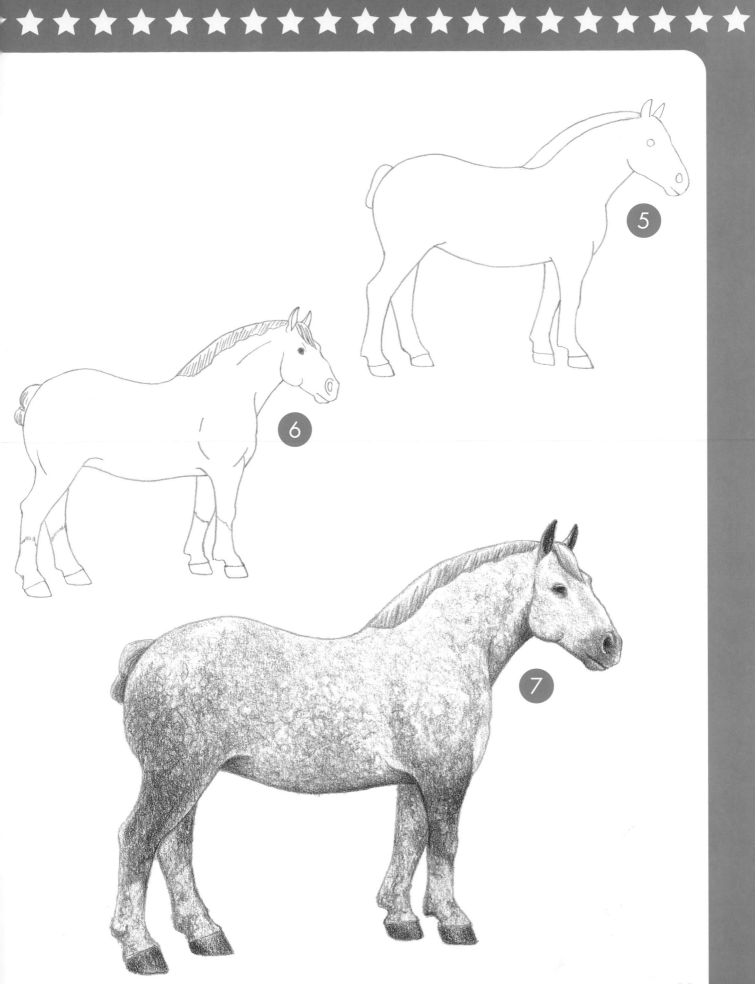

Pony of the Americas

This **polka-dotted** pony has a two-toned mane and a long, arched neck. Draw its spotted coat with circles and ovals.

1

2

3

4

5

fun fact

In 1954, an Iowan breeder named Les Boomhower discovered the unique coat of a foal born with an Arab/Appaloosa mother and a Shetland father. This foal was the first Pony of the Americas, a breed developed for children to show and ride.

Tennessee Walking Horse

With its ultra-smooth walk, this gaited horse is a proud show-ring competitor with a sweet, gentle personality.

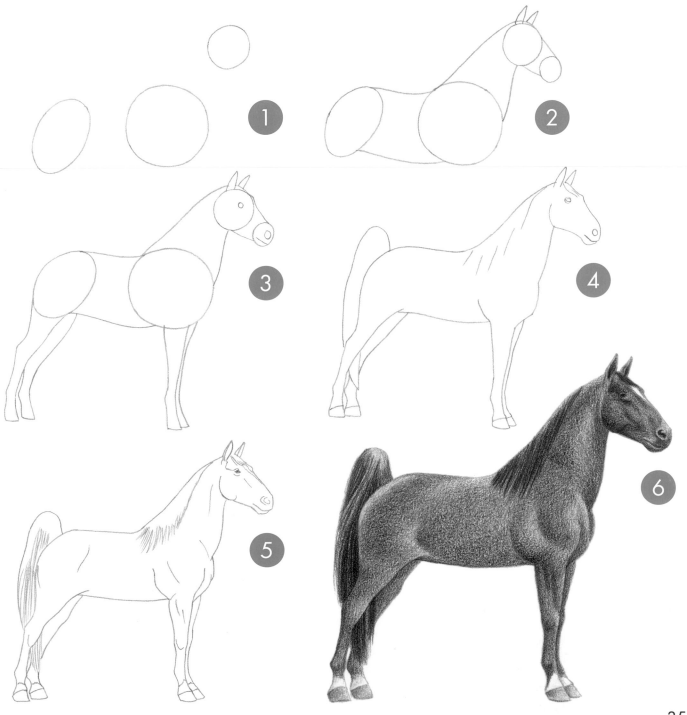

Dutch Warmblood

Although it's not as **tall** as its mother, the legs on this **athletic** foal are already nearly as long and almost as strong as hers!

fun fact

Most horses are registered according to their ancestry. For example, if a horse has a registered mother (dam) and father (sire), it's considered to be that breed. But the Dutch Warmblood has an "open" studbook. So regardless of its ancestry, a Dutch Warmblood foal is never automatically accepted for registration. Every foal must first be inspected for breed-worthiness!

Rocky Mountain Pony

Its dappled **chocolate** coloring and **creamy** mane
and tail make this pretty pony a one-of-a-kind sensation!

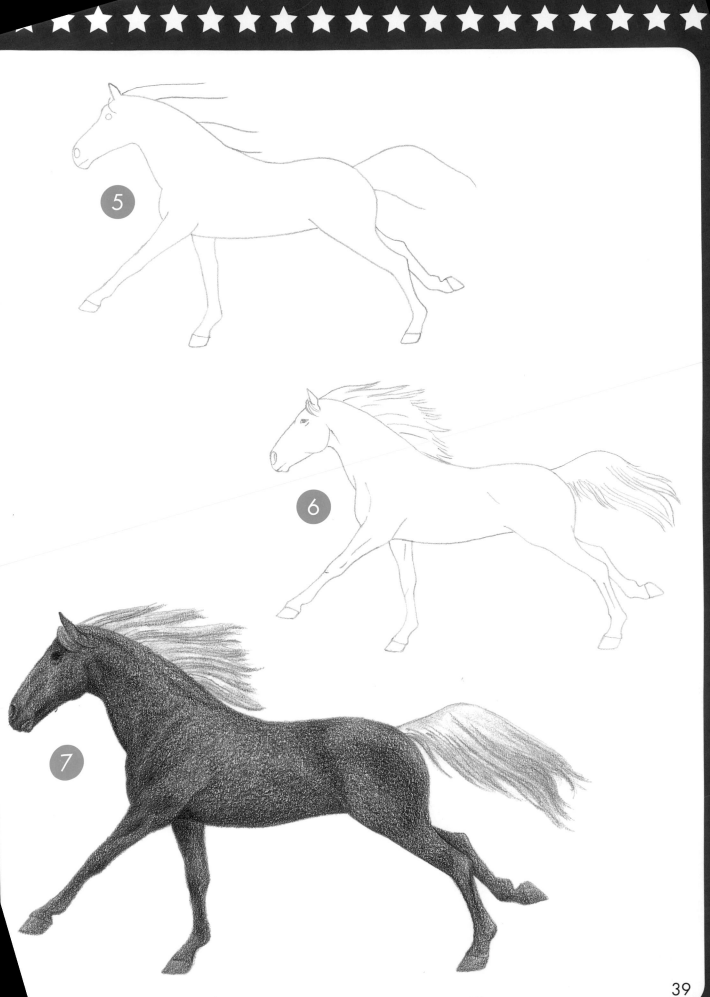

Andalusian

This **noble** breed is a fabulous **gymnast,** just like its descendants: the famous "dancing" white Lippizaners of Vienna.